RECKLESS PILGRIMS

Also by Allison Thorpe

Thoughts While Swinging a Wild Child in a Green Mesh Hammock
Swooning and Other Art Forms
What She Sees
Dorothy's Glasses
The Shepherds of Tenth Avenue

RECKLESS PILGRIMS

Poems by
Allison Thorpe

Broadstone

Library of Congress Control Number 2020950306
ISBN 978-1-937968-79-3

Text Design & Typesetting by Larry W. Moore

Cover Artwork & Design by Stephanie Potter

Broadstone Books
An Imprint of
Broadstone Media LLC
418 Ann Street
Frankfort, KY 40601-1929
BroadstoneBooks.com

For Richard and Taura
And in memory of Russell Estes who started our journey

We are all pilgrims in search of the unknown.
Paulo Coelho

Contents

I

Iris

Stone Ruins, Slater's Field

Reckless pilgrims, we came to the land,
bearing our hunger like a bony heart,
our ragged dreams an open sea.

We thought the stone ruins just local color
the country realtor wove into our purchase,
history altered to myth for the selling:
a rock foundation of a house burned down
generations ago, and fifty paces out, a graveyard.
We tentatively surveyed the ridges and valleys,
uncovering only stinging nettles and beggars lice.
Boundaries had shifted with seasons, weeds bulldozing
fence and flower, the land's slow ache of redressing.

We wallowed in the stories: two old women alone,
luring a preacher to their bed, burying bricks of gold,
witching water from dry wells during a strawberry moon.
That the women kept a still near Gooselick Creek,
hauled corn and sacks of sugar at daybreak, stashed
bottles in a tree stump, a ditch, a shallow cave.

The base of the house when we found it proved
a poor crumbling limestone enclosure wild mainly
in honeysuckle and mayapple rumor. The remains
of a charred and jagged chimney jutted skyward.
The wind spilled no voices to the hush, no flow
of cosmic connection, surely no answer to legend.

Past the hill, I stumbled over the first headstone;
then we saw the rest -- a crooked fairyland
circle under the cool umbrella of maple;
lichen-graffitied grey stone crops like loose
roughened teeth of some giant lain to rest.
Myrtle soothed the soil like prayer.

In that cathedral of uncertain shadow, we spoke
in hushed tones of clearing the old house site,

weaving fresh flowers among the graves;
but a sudden breeze bristled the blossoms,
ropy grapevine gnarled a jealous embrace,
and something unseen settled us to silence,
something not quite like benediction.

To the Boy I Remember, the Man I Came to Love

Born to country, you understood
the sharp scent of the hunt,
a keening of hatchet and knife,
the wade of trail and stream:
qualities, also, for war.

When your number came up,
I wondered if I would ever see you again.
What we had suddenly suspended,
insignificant, distant, easily forgotten,
your parting kiss eager and patriotic
and so full of somewhere else.

You came home quiet,
Da Nang, Ho Chi Minh, Saigon,
just names dropped from a reporter's lips,
stained memories buried
in an old documentary of your mind.

You never talked about what happened—
no leeches, no malaria, no blood—
preferred instead singing to ponds
patriotic with fish,
whispering to children
eager to tie knots or name trees,
burying black iris bulbs in the field,
then softly pining their return.

NOISY BIRDS

After Jim Wayne Miller's "The Bee Woman"

She loved their clash and jangle,
loved the idea that all things
did not have to be beautiful,
but that beauty lived in all things.
To her it wasn't noise: the girl
who couldn't carry a birthday tune
delighted in these discordant
singers and ratcheted chanters.
They kept the seasons in motion,
stated their feelings upfront,
echoed the world into reason.

One summer distant relatives
(on their way from somewhere
to somewhere else) camped the
night, awoke sore and grumbling,
wanted to know what machine
had been working all night.
A whippoorwill, she said;
but they disputed her, thought
she'd lost her mind, declared
she'd been in the country too long.

The guinea hens roamed wherever
they wanted, hurrying paths beaten
through tall grass and under brush,
their sinewy grey and white speckled
rowdiness heralding danger, grating
ghosts, begging wheat berries,
then moving on. Their squawking
was like the grating latch of her
childhood opening and closing
and then opening again.

The blue jay never stopped calling
"thief." What had she stolen?
His land with a tractor?
His tree with a chainsaw?
Did he look upon her like she
viewed the new-paved roads
and great sagging power lines?
His bright and crested
politics keeping her grounded
to the causes and stations
of life's subtle worth.

Were her poems and stories
then just off-key jarrings,
a sort of melodic cacophony,
and she some machine
that went steady, steady
all through the night
pounding words onto paper,
thoughts and feelings to lines,
crying thief to time and passion?
Had those birds once been foreign
elements swooping to strange
land as she had done, their
voices never quite settling
to harmony, but ones so
well-fitted to the song?

ZSA ZSA AND THE HARMONY OF PUDDLES

We were cutting up the peach tree;
The storm last night took it.

Slain monster fallen now
After a wet and windy battle.

The sun, impulsive, breaks cloud,
Washes our faces as if in apology,

A trade off in one of those
Giveth and *taketh away* moments.

Neighbors call this soggy ground "rotten."
You, gone so long, rejoice each squishy step.

After chores, we sprawl in the gazebo
Not wanting to release the day,

Linked to spirit's renewal,
Wonder of sense and form—

The inhaled creed of lilacs,
Witness of a faithful moon—

Feasting each breath as first,
Lusting each sigh as last.

Zsa Zsa, glad we are out and about,
Barks her jubilation

(An accented yelp you always said),
Then dashes to a puddle and drinks her fill.

Snowmelt or rain, her preference,
Ignoring her full dish.

Maybe she smells the chlorine,
The cityness of the water we provide.

Maybe she races from puddle to puddle
As if she too might lose the taste of earth.

CHICORY BLUES

It was hot August lonely.
Even the power left us
in the dim of candles.
Even the moon refused to
come out of her cool dark cave.
Even the dog has gone
to live with the neighbor cows
in their shriveled pond.

We walk the baked dust
of an early lane,
sleep-mugged zombies
hoping for relief.
Cresting the hill,
we see spread before us
an ocean of wild chicory tufts
rising from the ditches
in filigreed blue glory.

Weedy and forgotten
most days,
but here, now,
they flow unbridled,
a lusty quell of color,
divine deception,
damping this fevered land.

Old Enemies

Your faded camouflage shirt,
fresh from sun and air,
but scented still of
jungles and decay,
carrying the crease
of some sharp-eyed certainty
slung over your shoulder
that I cannot iron out.

Every washday I regard
the shirt warily, consider
reporting it missing,
mixing it with the Goodwill,
surrendering it to some
trashcan, burying forever
its ingrained rigid shape,
the rinse and dried dream.

You wore it when we met.
A shirt of abstracts, you said:
love and hate,
duty and honor,
life and death,
justice for all.

The rips are stitched now
like scars, the patches
fraying and familiar
as your darker days.
No softening can penetrate
that starched remembrance.

Again, I fluff, fold,
tuck its fragile life
back into a drawer—
renewed treaty—
earned freedom
to be worn again.

Forget Your Sunday Morning Deer

After Al Stewart's "Sunday Morning Deer"

Forget your Sunday morning deer
and the rest of the week deer as well.

If they kept to their deer meadow
we would be happy.

Instead they forage my beans and lettuce,
chomp their way through kale and spinach,

gobble impatiens and growing hosta plants,
feast on delicate rosebuds before they even open,

kick apart the stone wall
we so carefully built of river slate,

send their best athletes to scale
the ever rising wire fences.

One day I expect to see them
dancing among the sweet potato vines,

martini glasses in their hooves,
lamp shades dangling antlers,

gorging and munching their cocktail hour
until we run screaming back to the city,

abandoning the mulched and fertile ground
to drift back, untamed, in triumph.

Circe in October

Gathered on this grassy knoll,
a family split, now together,
sore memories behind us,
future as smooth as this
autumn day so blue and warm.
We could be Odysseus and crew
back from the Trojan War,
lured by the land before us--
Circe singing her enticements,
her maids called catalpa
and acacia and persimmon
bow and sweep frocks of
gold and red and orange,
offer the dark wine,
the purpled fruit.
Circe bestows her banquet
before us trying to transform
our will to the more basic
shapes where we root
about her feet for acorns.

We stay at a distance,
for we know her story.

Still, we do not leave.

Finding us there later
in the spume-scattered sun,
she cloaks us in the skirts
of her sweet silken night
and sails us homeward.

Last Night, the War Escaped

your skull
a broken
dark deception

legs twitching
some far-flung
race for life

throat
a gargled
well

clenched fists
weapons
still unleashed

I soothe
the battle
from your brow

wrap my arms—
gentle sentries—
to ease invasion

sweeten the ear
with a whispered   ***
here   now   these peaceful hills

FALL CARNIVAL

All the summer music makers
prove tireless performers today—
crickets, tree frogs, cicadas—
tricked as this late
October afternoon
wraps loving and lazy
like a balmy blanket,
some masked spectacle
enticing us with beads and masks.

Playful wrens swing
from autumn's gold
to maple's scarlet clamor
in this dash of illusion.

Clouds juggle an aging sky;
the parading sun—
bone-cozy marvel—
its spellbinding charisma.

White tailed deer prance
their skittish scrunch and crackle
among chatty pine cones,
leaf-rowdy residue.

Even the forsythia—
simple believer—
tumbles its yellow harmony
onto the lane like street theater.

In my shirt sleeves,
pleasured wonder to step and mind,
taming the frantic
thoughts of future hours
with this cotton candy day,
I'm an easy mark:

eager,
even joyous,
to be fooled.

The Sage on This Raw Day Reminds Me of William Faulkner

The herb garden runs
        in rags and tatters;
it is my fault for
        letting things go wild.
All the old verities gone:
        the sage is dying.
Year after year it reigned,
        roots far-flung and deep.
No matter the winter,
        it welcomed spring in fuzzy
green hurrah; but slowly
        the sage was crowded out
by the low creepers, roving
        gangs of mint and thyme,
feisty outlanders:
        oregano, chamomile, horehound.

Sage, your charming southern
        manner has got you nowhere.
Miss Emily, Jenny, Dilsey—
        Faulkner was right—
the old women held the world
        together with silly things
like politeness and propriety,
        that sturdy wisdom
now bowed in hollow
        eccentricity.
Your dress drapes quietly
        in a closet somewhere.
Leaves like grey hair
        litter an earthy pillow.

A Government of Snow

A government of snow has raged
across this peaceful countryside,
white tongued filibuster gusting overrule,
gristly congress of flakes,
taxing even the most hospitable among us.

House pipes froze, ice snapped power lines,
and the goats blared their displeasure to the moon.
It seemed all we did was carry firewood
from shed to stove, dry out mittens and boots
tainted with flurried propaganda.

Reading by the flick of candlelight,
counting daffodils instead of sheep,
we cluster warmth of bodies, ideas,
under such an oppressive regime,
eager to stuff spring's ballot.

How like a Dumbwaiter is Early Spring

Hauling our mechanical hearts
        Our hopeful freight
                Into another fickle season

Unknown hand at the controls
        This random rise and fall
                Through wither and bloom

Once more
        The birds' bitter
                Chatter wakes us

Into their chorus
        A stolen spring
                Weaves its story

No happy release
        For lingered notes
                Tucked to breast

Shored dreams
        Of stirring worm
                And bathing puddle

Promised warmth
        Snatched cruelly
                Back to zero

We watch blushing
        Trees caught with
                Their blossoms showing

Our breath
        A tongueless sigil
                Blobbing windows

Reluctant daffodils
        Festoon themselves
                In snowy bows

Even the dog's
        Rimy muzzle
                Begs forgiveness

Chair huddled
        And grim eyed
                We chew hope

As the sun teases deliverance
        Somewhere a tree learns
                The language of leaves

Nature's Child

The young Bullfinches in their party coloured Raiment
bustle about among the Blossoms & poise themselves like
Wire dancers or tumblers, shaking the twigs & dashing off
the Blossoms.

Dorothy Wordsworth

Daughter of peace
born of the great war,
married to a protested war,
grandmothered in an unnecessary war,
I still search for that core of quietness,
that connection you express
so easily in your journals,
discovering self
in mirrored lake,
solitary island,
a frolic of birds.

What would you make
of all this violence, Dorothy,
the school shootings,
the random explosions
this new world of wild?
You found unruliness
in landscapes
shot full of violets,
random explosions of primrose,
the violence of a thunderstorm.

I tried to get away
from the world too,
but the world found me.
Now there is no real place to hide.
I am left to look for peace
in the touch of a child,
the grace of soil sunwarm and yielding
and eager for sprout,
a greening ravel heading home.

II

DANDELION

Huddled Masses

For days, chainsaws have shaken
the new spring air, each breath
a gasp of oil and sawdust.
Loggers have moved in
like feuding neighbors
to these unworried hills.

In the twilight cool,
I stumble the battered earth,
unwilling observer to this tragedy.
A tangle of budding briar
abandoned to ditch voices mission,
blooms one clear epiphany.

With wheelbarrow and shovel,
I strike, frantically freeing
the endangered natives:
the royalty—
Queen Anne's lace and jewelweed,
fragile beauties—
coneflower and wood violet,
the commoners—
ox-eye daisy and daylily.

Some are shunted to sunset,
others by moonlight,
all before the tyranny
of dozer and backhoe.
The dog keeps guard.
Tired, hungry, yearning
for a bed, we trudge
this overland route.

At dawn's edge,
I inspect their settling,
still as a statue

in some distant harbor.
Freshly rooted, watered,
the transplants sprawl
their new liberty, the sun
a lamp lifted.

Notes from the Farm

You come and go
　　like bees or rain drops,
　　　　this broken hilltop breeze.

Forget seconds or seasons!
　　Time is your rapid heart on my lips,
　　　　the questing reach of a cold bed.

The road, adventure,
　　those are your mistresses
　　　　I struggle in the hush of absence.

I pot basil, store winter squash,
　　search clouds on wind-torn days.
　　　　Wayward blue jays comfort me.

Most days a glad cadence
　　of chores, family, friends,
　　　　other men

who patch a fence
　　share a glass of wine.
　　　　Nothing more.

I am Eve strolling the garden,
　　Annie Oakley riding the hills,
　　　　Penelope weaving
　　　　　　. . . weaving.

BLACKBERRIES

Doused in anger
You have gone
To pick blackberries
Spewing the trailed air
With your raging motes

I want to say that anger
Will translate
To the fruit you touch
Will eventually sour
The fragrant jam
Maybe crack the jelly jars
Spreading the spidery lines

I want to say this heat
That burdens your brow
Used to tangle our nights
Scorch the pleasured arch
Of back and thigh
Drip from our skin
In sweltered delight

I want to say that fever died
One October morning
When the geese honked overhead
Or when I cleaned
The dust bunnies
From beneath the table
But the date escapes me

I want to say I'm sorry
And wave to where you are
Across this field
Of healthy green
Hope to get more

Than a tatter of smile
More than just two distant sailors
With nothing in common
But the dark sea between

CHASING THE LITTLE DOG I NAMED JIMMY

Chasing the little dog I named Jimmy
wasted most of a busy morning.

It started when he wormed his way
into the chicken coop barking

biddies from their warm nesting.
He had never experienced rooster spurs before.

His yelps trailed down the holler
and I thought I was rid of him.

In the middle of baking bread
I saw him trying to dig up the mole

that was plaguing my green bean patch,
loose dirt spraying the air like an oil gusher.

I shooed him off to the woods
where he eyed me suspiciously:

he was only trying to help
his white-freckled face seemed to say.

Feeling sorry for the little stray,
I brought out a bowl of milk-soaked bread,

but he was having none of it.
When I looked through the window

a bread rising later,
it was all gone,

and he was on top of the compost heap
scattering rinds, bones, corn cobs.

Scolding my foolishness for feeding him,
I drove him scampering once more.

Whose spirit was he
to torment me like this?

An old boyfriend?
Some Yankee in-law?

The squirrel I accidentally
ran over last spring?

He reminded me of the mule
our neighbor spent years training

before he lost his edge
and mellowed to hand and harness.

Late afternoon I saw Jimmy racing the yard,
a host of uprooted pansies in his mouth.

This time he thought my chase
a game new and wonderful.

He scrabbled to the top of the wood pile
sending logs and pansies flying.

As I tried to restack the firewood,
I saw him tugging the mesh around the new apple tree.

I considered the BB gun,
but he cocked his head

as if to innocently ask
aren't you having fun yet?

He gave a soft warm whimper
and took a few paces toward me.

With melting heart and brain,
I refilled the bread and milk dish.

The next morning he and the food were gone.
I watched for him all day

and the weeks to come,
but he had moved on,

wandering, possibly lost,
a poem haunting these hills.

Heat

At first it feels so fine—
balmy fingers of air
massaging knotted bones,
loosing what is left
of winter's clutch.

Soon plant edges
begin to tattle,
spreading their yellow
and brown gossip
around the neighborhood.
You don't want to believe,
but it shimmers and curls
the corners of your heart.

The blistering swells go on forever,
Frost's world ending in fire not ice.
You stare now beyond the heat
and wonder if you can
feng shui the clouds,
wonder longer of things
you should have done:
paint the dresser,
read the book your mother got you,
white water rafting,
one more night with the banjo boy.

The world is stale,
motionless.
You push the porch swing,
prod the wind chimes,
twirl, spin, stomp,
hoping to start a chain reaction.
You stretch out your hand,
a beggar seeking alms:
the crust of breeze,
sweet wine of rain.

COMMON WEALTH

After Wendell Berry's "The Peace of Wild Things"

My sister is killing dandelions.
Actually, she hugs the checkbook
while we busily loiter
her front picture window
and watch a uniformed man
spray the yellow blooms.
I want to turn away, but can't,
as one does at an accident
or when a funeral passes.
She glows; once again
her lawn will echo
that of neighbor
and the perfect stretch
beyond.

Later,
I toast them at dinner:
    To the dandelions!
I have savored the greens in spring,
rubbed their buttery softness
on my laughing daughter's nose,
enjoyed the wine with friends,
whispered their soft spore to wind.
My sister raises her glass:
    Good riddance!

When I leave the next morning,
a few straggled smears
of brown weakly
nod a farewell.
The crisp air clinches
a whiff of poison
I try not to breathe as I pass.

That evening,
nuzzled on porch swing,
I inhale the glazed and rosy

musk of homecoming.
My neighbors, oak and hickory,
creak and sigh in welcome hymn,
cardinals pleasure the dimming air,
deer snort faintly down the hill.
The last folds of sun highlight
dandelions that pepper the view,
join wild onion and wood violet,
switch grass and beech fern
in this harmony of voice,
this wonder of difference
that is our place in the world.

WHAT TO LOVE AFTER DAFFODILS

For Juanita

The sky, surely,
its dappled confessions,

any dirt road that runs off
into a dark binge of cedars,

hawk shadow ghosting
foxglove and lemon basil,

an old barn singing dust
like a hymn to sunshine,

the chink and jangle
of porch chimes,

hummingbirds sparking
their sheen of jewels,

limestone bluffs that preen
rivered reflections,

the rampant prophesy of lilacs,
hoot owl's nightly sermons,

your wooden chair still
rocking the empty hours,

and, yes, even the faces
dampening the shoveled dirt,

their slow burn of prayer,
that promise while we sleep.

Lullaby Bridge

Civil War soldiers crossed this bridge,
marched the wooden planks
with dutiful optimism.

From where I sit,
leaning against the rusty crosspieces,
dangling my legs
over the rolling water,
I can almost feel the vibrations,
the trample of rallied feet,
hear hooves slap timbers,
brave fathers, brothers, lovers
who waved goodbye,
uncertain of return.

Once a covered wooden bridge,
burned then rebuilt,
witness to blood and battle.
Today, the iron trestle warms with sun.
The river rocks quietly,
purring its day,
hypnotic in its indifference.
It cares little for war or bridge,
has no language for goodbye
or the ebb and flow of love.

Every time you leave,
I wonder if you will return.
This bridge the span of our lives:
metal's infinite patience,
wood's splintered soul.

Cold Coffee

It's not

> like milk fresh and smooth
> and icy on the palate
> or frosty snowflakes
> that tickle the tongue
> or clear spring water
> savored from a tin cup

It's more
> like the chill of your mouth
> caressing my lips
> the quickened gulp
> of some dark drowning

A Rest of Peaches

I have been canning peaches all morning
Sorting the plump fuzzy fragrances
Readying water and utensils
The plunge and scald
And plunge again to ice
To remove the skin
Then halving and pitting
Filling clean jars
With sweet and lemon
To hold the brightness
Water bathing the due time
Removing jars with tongs
The welcome ping of seal

I lie now in a hammock
Resting like the peaches
Cooling in the kitchen
Dreaming the joy come winter
Hand lifting a jar off the shelf
To thaw the ice-bone season
Relish that heart
Of summer gleaming

Inertia, Contemplated

After Robert Morgan's "Inertia"

There is confederacy afoot.
Vandals have waged conflict with the wood beyond
my west window: lipstick orange screams slashed
across sassafras and oak, gold paint flecked everywhere.

Look! To the east!
Someone has torched the distant maple grove.
There are things still I want of those lands—
nut and berry, root and herb, hoot and song.

But there! And there!
Limbs shook, leaves down and scuffed to a dirty
humus brown, littering the earth in elemental protest.
Is it too late for a fall garden?

Whose rebellion is this?
Only some plucky northern remembrance would dare
storm my southern outlook. I am only a bit slow
in dawning this bright morning of ice-rimmed alarm.

What happened to plans so pure?
Items unchecked upon the list? Were they waylaid
by wolves? Insurance salesmen? Ailing babies? A day
or two lost lying in meadows with my thoughts too long?

Those ideas were good company!
It is only sometimes now that slumber nudges my night
with stray ghouls, bridges falling, ferris wheel demise;
and I wake and walk, nursing their stale validity.

So what happens? I drowse late.
Caught in quilts womb warm and a hint musty of sleep's
tongue, pillow dented perfectly, hair cascading midnight;
lain dormant so long vagrants think this spot uninhabited.

Listen! Are those bugles?
I step from bed and wrap the chill as an old robe, leave
the waltzing winter sleep to bear and squirrel, spark mass
and matter once more, teaching gravity the art of rising.

Deviations

Caught off guard
With October still
Styling the calendar.

Papers to be written
Hover like buzzards:
Black, hungry.

Leaves and letters
Scatter, resistant
To frantic rake.

Scrambling blindly
As light fails,
I turn—

One-eyed candles wink.
Vivaldi sails shadow.
You have laid the hearth.

My fire, leaping
From brain to branch,
Ignites.

Kentucky Crows

I have known them through every season:
black holes ripping winter's stunning lace,

slashes of midnight hovering spring,
gossipers pecking the eyes from summer;

but it is here—on this mist lonely
November day as they swoop pine to willow,

bob cedars hobbled from last year's ice,
rude showers to earth, that I see their fit,

their ragged jigsaw so vital to grayness,
outline not as startling against fog,

harsh omen muted in the barren density,
their distant revelry a winsome party

to which I have not been invited.

40 Days

Fall's rain will not stop.
A low sky glooms its marrow,
heaves its stuffing like a Christmas goose.

Our crayon box crammed with dark,
then a shock of salmon,
yellow on its way to dying.

Lingered pansies surrender their delights,
turn limp purple faces our way,
beg to be let inside.

No longer a friend, wind
clatters the glass for entry,
paws like a seething grizzly

as birches fury limbs on roof:
demented drummer boys
thrashing fearsome tempos.

We worry shutters, sandbags,
aardvarks and zebras marching in pairs,
their weathered invitations.

Barring the latch,
we abandon our eggnog,
reach for anyone's hand.

Patchwork

The only anniversary he remembered,
and she often wondered if an accidental
purchase had coincided the occasion.

But there he stood--the gifted quilt
an outrageous abstraction of reds
and purples and oranges and pinks,
the scraps a mismatched discordance
hand-stitched by some old woman
who lived "three hollers over."

Through the years it proved strong,
just sun and wind to fluff its fate,
sweetly cozying their winters,
falling more familiar to the eye.

When he died she wrapped herself
in its folds, the clash of color
an unlikely sanity, the tender
gather, oh, such loving arms!

Flashback Orange

The fruit is like yesterday
when you think of him.
Safest to roll it around
in the palm for awhile,
ponder the unbroken circle,
soften the waxy reality.
Say it is easier to open that way.
Slowly sink your teeth to skin,
shuddering the familiar rush.
Pretend you are Hemingway in Paris;
relish hunger like Cezanne,
rejoicing each small truth
as layers exposed to air.
Cast peels to fire,
one by pungent one
like a long list
of forgotten desires.
Linger the remembered
taste upon the tongue.
Hallow the sweet flesh.
Let all the wild juices
baptize what is left of love.

III

Lilac

Crocus in Snow

We nub our lure to light
Earthy womb behind our waking

Quilted layers shrug
The herald of an icy floor

Beautiful, we rise
Open our purple robes

To flash the world
Shameless in our season

Duet for Zsa Zsa and the Repairman

The mower quit
so I called Jim Dyson.
Spark plugs, he thought.

Maybe it was old eyes,
or a trick of the sun.
or some familiar movement,
but Zsa Zsa, trotting
out of the woods,
old bone in her mouth,
saw him
bent over the machine
and thought it was you.

Buried treasure forgotten,
she raced his way,
a strange caterwauling
of welcoming yips and yowls.
It wasn't until he turned
and said, "Hey, pup"
that she realized
her mistake,
ears flattened
slinking off, confused,
back to her bone,
something in the world
not right.

I thought of the times
I spotted a dark haired figure
at the end of the grocery aisle,
a blue pea coat in the crowd,
the flash of a vehicle
in the drive.

I wished I had a bone.

In the Budding Green

In the budding green
and awakened air of morning

when the days blush
and the fat hills preen themselves

I will look for you
just beyond the far woods

where the Deptford pinks
strut and sway their lyrics

where red fox will perk her ears
to man or gun or kit

where the wild crab smears
its fragrant mysteries

and the moon entices
the vanished from their hiding

CLIMB

Somewhere in Kentucky a forsythia
offers its yellow echo to the sun.

A long-haired woman haunts a window,
wonders what to do with an hour,

how to outlast the day,
follows a jet's silver glint in the dull sky.

She opens the curtain to more light,
but only questions wash the room.

How often do we look up
for warmth, beauty, answers?

Do we ache the bird's easy wing,
the chic of God's tongue

as we propel ourselves
into the star-blind wild,

dreaming that vast
and oh so incredible blue?

THE DISSONANCE OF MUGWORT

Around and around
     with shoveled invasion
         I traverse its ragged
             boundaries as a spell
cast and followed.
     Once just a slip
         of an herb, it stands
             now gnarled and woody,
mooselike in attitude,
     bullying thyme and chive,
         gone too far in its
             obsession, troth
too deep in stead.
     A snip in the pillowcase
         to stir dream I was told,
             but I need no aid to visions.

Around and around
     I slice and dig,
         helped by rain
             and dog to unearth
its monstrous claim.
     Too great for wheelbarrow,
         its crown is pulled
             from grasp, roped and
hauled down the hollow
     to rule some northern slope.
         By moon I see the scar,
             slash of dark earth
sewn and settled,
     tongue of spice
         ghosting
             the ravished air.

CHIAROSCURO
(PHOTO ON THE NIGHTSTAND)

There is art
to how my arm lies
along your shoulder
the invisible arc
between bodies
how the still hand
curves neck
with such ease

a cigarette
forever burning
in your fingers
the smoke more real
than life
as it stuffs the room
with shadowy linger

bright faces
catch happiness
chime the hour
of cruel
and beautiful

Awake
my sun blind fingers
search the hollow bed
seeking weight
composition
palette of flesh

ALL DAY GEESE HAVE DANCED

After Effie Waller Smith's "Preparation"

All day geese have danced
The sky in fluid tattoo
Honking their winter gossip

While I hauled and stacked firewood to shed
Rushed apples and pumpkins to root cellar
Tossed mulch on tulip and gladiola bulbs

The dog under foot at every turn
Eyes questioning such hasty nonsense
My all work and no play

I sit finally and rub her ears
Her tail telling me I chose wisely
That life seeks pause in preparation

With a heart usually spring fed
I admit delight in the fall flaunting
The sky symphony and tree art

Drink in the sun's clouded concoctions
Before night paints its plush fortune
Onto our silent contentment

WINDOW

You the Widder Woman?
The handyman shuffled
out of his faded pickup truck.
Cheek packed with chaw,
he sent a rusty arc of spittle
toward the forsythia bush.
His gaze openly examined me:
the grey streaks, wrinkles,
garden grubby overhauls.
I wondered if he would part
my lips to check my teeth.
He scanned my house and land,
pale eyes already seeing himself
lazing in the green hammock,
grabbing a fat chicken
for the stewing pot,
opening the refrigerator
to check if there was any beer.

Little lady like you
shouldn't have to keep
up a house, all this land.
His arm swept air
as if he were clear cutting trees,
calculating how much money
that cut lumber could bring.
Little lady like you
should have a man around
for stuff like this.
He closed one eye
in what I took to be a wink.
I wanted to tell him to get lost
but I needed a new window
and the leaves had already turned
the corner toward winter.

I retreated to what was left
of the fall flowers, worked
mulch over spent ground,
trying to ignore his leer
until he finished.

I watched his truck belch
its way down the drive,
then threw down my rake and gloves
with shaking hands.

I perched on a rock
overlooking the valley—
lavish in its autumn patchwork—
and searched for answers:
the sun's warming blood
coursed through my veins,
the hills cradled their iron
around my bones.

And Then One Day She Lost Poetry

Oh, not like the eyeglasses or keys
that mysteriously meander
their way into the freezer

or the running shoe
puppy-chomped and spit-soggy
wedged under the bed

More like the sun-speckled trout
snapping filament, flipping tail,
and racing for open waters

the last parking meter coin
slithering from hand and rolling
toward the muck-mawed sewer grates

a country wet with promise
suddenly hung out to dry
like some red-blotched wash of negativity

She didn't notice when poetry left
just one morning her tongue thickened
lifeless as mossed quarry stone

The clouds were no help
no castle or dragon shapes anywhere
only vague fuzz linting the horizon

Even the sun seemed to taunt her
disappearing like a plump-winked eye
a ripe cherry bitten by birds

She leaves the windows open now
just in case a moony night
coughs up a shooting star or comet

Some random spore rangy and wild
that might catch in the lacy blue curtains
or land on her idle tongue
and give it ease

Nothing Was Random

Nothing was random, the footprints
a deliberate stalking across my lower field,
around the hydrangea remnants
to peek the undersides of the porch,
a close circle of woodshed,
twice around the house,
down the outdoor cellar steps and back up again.

I put off my morning chores
and followed the melting tracks,
examining the widened impressions.
Not deer or squirrel.
Maybe the draggled dog that lived down the road.
Raccoon a possibility.
Hopefully not wolf or bear
or the bobcat I heard last spring.

I felt an insane urge to laugh.
The tracks tied me suddenly to the living:
an old woman by herself
among this remote expanse.
For an instant they made my solitude
a community of sociable nature
before casting a deliberate hook
of unease upon the day.

I brushed snow from the truck,
shoveled the pathway,
loaded up the wood bin.
While scattering crumbs for the birds
I nervously looked off into the distance.
Was it watching me?
Studying my seasoned bones
for their wildness?

An Old Revolutionary Gets Through Winter

For Ed McClanahan

By thinking of it as a time to regroup,
To dwell the celebration of old victories,
Hoist a glass or two of the mellowed grape,
Dormant but for fireplace rebellion,
Holed up quite nicely away from the cold
Long-winded politics brewing outside.

But plotting, always plotting—
How to capture more ground, negotiate
Weeds, stave the hunger of blight;
Readying tools: steely allies; scouting
Seeds to germination; letting garden
Catalogs be all the propaganda needed.

By inspecting the colorful troops that line
Basement shelves—honey, peaches, beans,
Tomatoes still saluting a loyal redness,
Blackberries huddled like foreign converts.

By marching to the discipline of words
That bow to this wooded world of snowy hills;
By musing the mischief of their spirit,
Reveling in the legend of their reign.

THE LION AND THE LAMB

The old house has finally fallen.
I knew it was coming.

The windows were first to go,
random targets of nomadic boys.

The door went next, taken possibly
by someone who needed a door, or firewood.

Then the roof, caving sharply like
some giant foot had stomped in anger.

Now, today, after raw winds and rain,
it lies, a shriveled mound of jagged lumber,

splinter and nail concoction
amidst the first breath of spring,

eerie March contrast
to the joyous yard, a blaze

of divine yellow and white,
hyacinth, jonquils, forsythia,

crocus purpling the new-sprung grass,
the blooms a colorful hallelujah

for what has gone, for those
who lovingly gave them birth.

Sand Hill Cranes

You hear them in the wings
though you cannot see them yet,
a gentle gurgle
you long to detect,
thinking they have some
crooning wisdom to impart:
career forecast,
winning lottery number,
ancient knowledge we once had
but lost to weeds,
hoping they will give us a hint
and lead us back.
This crisp February morning
you stop your walk in the field—
even the dog pauses
her eager snuffling—
then they appear
in a vee flying south,
flying north,
back and forth they weave,
raising hope,
dashing it
now into a line
like showgirls swaying
their plumy bodies,
long legs on display.
You want them to be returning.
You want the groundhog
to be right this time.
Hypnotic higher power,
do they see
this silent and childlike,
this believing audience?

Thinking of Aung San Suu Kyi While Smelling the Lilacs

To bathe the boundless air once more,
the skin a joyous parchment,
hair now sister to wind.

Free of knitted chains, the hands dance.
Winter's arrest a history,
sun offers our open future.

The world has grown feral in our absence:
thistles thick as soldiers in the field,
quackgrass a general nuisance,

entrenched roots that require
generations of upheaval to abolish,
but daffodils have rioted the hillside,

crocus loyal their return,
wood violets chant a fragile
poetry among the undergrowth,

snowdrops dance milky dreams,
and here—the unruly lilac—
how sweet the revolution!

DECONSTRUCTING THE GOODBYE HOUSE

What came before merely
breath from winter's slick lips

caught in a streetlight's kiss
gone to icy canter.

You built the after
of quarry stone and oak,

then added a lifetime:
honeysuckle's rapid embrace,

a green theater of spreading hills,
the frisky yip of fox kits,

a red teapot on the shelf,
an overrun of lemon balm and oregano,

the sky on a good day,
a man named Joe,

loft-born babies, tools oiled and hung,
a quilt of scraps, maybe a snake or two,

peaches preening glass jars,
fusty leaves in autumn,

family gone to college, jobs, a field
of gravestones, the thinning air.

You pack what's left
of silence in an overnight bag,

close the latch one more
time, a dawning

fire at your back, the sift
of tender light through trees.

There is a road ahead,
and you have chosen its story.

IV

FORGET ME NOT

The Room Upstairs

It's the kind of place people abandon
the night before the rent is due,
a space where rain drops
in without being asked,
table tattooed with the smiles
of countless beer bottles,
bed the unwilling accomplice
of too many midnight confessions.
It's not what Virginia had in mind.

But the morning sun is kind
and the long windows open
onto the market street
where, weeks ago, an old woman
gave me a pot of ivy,
the strands cascading
like dark shiny hope.

Now, when I walk through
the door after mornings
writing at the local cafe,
my eyes hurry
to that green slash of life,
that earthy illusion of roots.

Telling Myself a Bedtime Story

The leaves have turned
Often since I left the garden

His absence held me
Too long to that land

I remained a bottomless well
A foot stuck in concrete

Until the delicious moon
Told me a secret one night

And I rolled off the mountain
Like a rabid pebble

My journal with its slobbering
Testimony followed me to this city

Where I sit at a wood desk
And try to write the rigid skyline

So foreign from my familiar pen
Of bendy willow and rebellious hills

Daily sirens now intrusive as a fly
In the next room who eventually

Finds an open window
And goes about its business

Car horns, some drunken couple in the street
The background music of my new night life

No more the questing owl
Or tree frog serenade

No distant coyote heralding kits
Or corn stalks wrestling the wind

No man coming along the river trail
Smiling with fish in hand

During the dark drug of sleep
The mind forgets such folly

But in the ramp of dream
The whippoorwill calls me

To the edge
Of almost there

THE PLUMB OF FORGETTING

Lose the string dangling a finger
         like some cheap party decoration

or an innocent peasant
         in a de Maupassant story

mask the gloom with zen-filled post-its
         waterfalls all spume and dazzle

bypass brain aerobics and mnemonics
         rust and dust will be your friends

blueberries   ginko biloba   salmon
         bury them in the yard one moon-bothered night

scissor that white t-shirt you sleep in
         the one still keening the room of him

then douse the velvet-wallowed darkness
         bless the stricken match

LIGHT AND HOW IT FALLS THROUGH WINDOWS

Every night a circus:

Strobe like a shameless barker
      spiels its blinding babble
           across the murky sky

Summer fireworks
      rainbow confetti
           over the distant field

Street signals
      juggle a constant
           red yellow green

Fire trucks
      whirl and spin
           their bright acrobatics

Dazzle the blue
      flickered magic
           of ambulances

Neon-crusted buildings
      hook the eye
           with gaudy lures

But I come from a dark country
      of hoot owl lullaby
           and coyote dream

Where night
      spends a single silver coin
           for entry

This new city thrums
      and lusters
           such a rich showy life

But the dull in me
         pines that past, that plain
              and stilling moon

EAVESDROPPING ON POETS AT THE COFFEE HOUSE

Each week the faithful:
tattoos and yoga pants,
thick dark-rimmed lenses,
rainbow hair that veils
faces already hard to read,
piercings like freckles,
voices flinging *fuck*
and *vagina* and *mollie*
with animated rage.

I write lilacs,
mourning doves,
tomatoes embarrassed on the vine,
lace collars and looking both
ways at crosswalks.
I am no one to them,
could be Anne Bradstreet
in my quaintness.

I reach for my cup,
coffee grown cold,
settle quiet in my chair
in case a whippoorwill—
something common
and familiar—
chants my name.

WILD, LATELY

This park bench: nothing
but a shaded haunting.
Birds fleck the trees,
tweet rumors of your absence.
I have become predictable,
as reckless these days as a tea cup,
as the tiered fountain that burbles
its recycled delight, happily
encased in a river of grey
concrete, a sparkling constant
of measured going nowhere.
Stiff signs beware our distance:
No Trespassing   Keep Out.

I close my eyes.
Think of rivers I once knew
that paid no mind to sign
or measure, welcomed gathers
of shoreline forget-me-nots,
the quiet stroke of fishers,
boys with rope swings,
the dangled toes of lovers.

To be like that water,
just some unruly thing
with no boundaries,
left to wander my own gush
and pull like a rogue tide.
To pilgrim the next luring
bend, sparkled, drenched,
in sun's echoed ravish.
To sing the cool drowning stars.

And Then There Were Tomatoes

Summer brags outside the tall windows
Inside, the air chatters winter

Our workshop assignment:
Describe something lost

Into this season of sun and longest days
I write about tomatoes

Planting them in my journal of absences
Their blooms caught between city lines

My pen a stick I poke
In the dirt of garden memories

How in our first year of not knowing
We filled row after hard worked row

With their leafy zest among wire enclosures
Dreaming the wealth of sauce and salad

Of sealing that lavish flame to jars
A primal passion to melt any snowy horizon

How soon those wire cages groaned
With the swell of animal wildness

The redness a blundered sea
With no hope of parting

Our lives became a slaking
An orbital glut of flesh and skin and seed

Even the chickens turned away
From our lavish offerings

Every measured garden after
Brought laughter for such innocence

But then we remembered that first ripeness
That plump of sun you placed

Childlike and warm into my hands
The mouth of summer singing

Petal, Falling

From my balcony, I see it drift dusk,
a glide and hover conjuring—
envy of artist, dancer, mime—

its purple and white down
a plush swoon of bird envy,
random elegance in a darkening world.

This city view of concrete and pipe
has little room for rogue nature,
some hobo pansy hitching a windy ride.

Fascinated mourners,
a pigeon and I watch
the petal's twirling drama

as I wish us all this luck:
a captive audience,
that elegant last dance.

SHE MISSES

. . . the language of lilacs,
those flowers gossiping poetry,
their sweet purple tongues
bewitching even the scarecrow in his work
and the dog dreaming the marrow from its bone.

. . . the way her fingers tasted
the earth, the nibble and bite
of that spicy dark loam,
savor of seed buried
only to gnaw its path to sun.

. . . the rugged green bouquet
of hills that blossomed her horizon,
perfumed rise of blue knoll,
the sniff of their sharp outline
wafting the distance to her porch swing.

. . . the metronomic caress
of the evening whippoorwill,
its musical embrace meant to spark
the waning stars and seize the plump
moon in its pulsing clutch.

. . . you, gone to ash these many years,
glimpsed walking among pine and oak,
a phantom presence dancing rain:
this long traveled love,
these spectral bones fleshing air.

MORE LIKE WOLF AND WILD OREGANO

This heat clings, a wanting
child unmoved by ice cream
and too far flung from sleep.

Air serious as a red
bandana soaked in steam
and draped over our mouths.

This city balcony
no porch of sweet
tea and rocking chair.

Hill breezes cannot
find me among this maze
of suffocating brick and steel.

Some nights are like that:
The body's red sweetness
in mismatched glasses,

wondering what star
will blaze our name,
what deep root
calls forth the bloom.

On Going Back Again

The familiar dirt road meanders
Like a sweet-ache dream
Through curve and creek
Shagbark hickories overhang their pleasure

The wide porch welcomes
Friends and cornbread
Peach pie gold in the crust
Hours charmed by music

Later, after the great beasts
Have culled the night
And even the whippoorwills
Cease their rusty mating

We rest on grassy blankets
Under a dazzled jabber
Of stars: our deep hearts
Marrowed in silence

We rest until the dew
Settles between our toes
And dawn-fed birds orchestrate
The melodies of our day

Return to Slater's Pond

Come June our soft feet would venture
      the pond's bottom: congregation of moldering leaves,
         fat pulp of algae, a few dusty catfish.

With every first dive into summer's cool drench,
      the slick silt and marl would clutch our toes
         like some clay-mouthed monster

before we thrashed back to the surface,
      scrabbling to tread water, heaving
         a direct course from dock to raft.

Gradually the sun's charm evaporated fears, settling
      the foundation of family, corn fields ripe
         for hiding, moon-spattered front porches.

The pond lies smaller these days of my visit,
      the uneven dock as close as I care
         to come to its sludge-flecked water,

battered planks of a raft float
      unconcerned among cattails and frogbit
         soon to be devoured by some land developer.

My history fashioned in every splash and gulp,
      weed bubbles now sob the surface of those summers.
      The sun bleeds for us all.

Songs in the Key of Darkness

Long before the city opens
its yawning rev and rumble,

and the sun is still snuggled
under horizon's dark blankets,

the birds send up
their festive invitations:

mantra of twittered gossip,
melodious zen enticements.

I sit on my balcony,
sleep a distant remembrance,

interrupted nightly by the dance
of worst case scenarios:

fever, fires, insane
men who rule the world.

The black sky soothes
the oppression of clouds.

With all that we have lost,
is it wrong to love these birds?

To feast upon
their joyous seeds of hope?

At the Liquor Store

I'm standing in a well distanced line
Cuddling my boredom-easing Chardonnay

When I see him walk in:
Blue scrubs   mask   bone-weary frame

He grabs some whiskey
Off the shelf without looking

I try to catch his eye
To thank him for all he's doing

To say I want to hug him
To let him know I pray for him

But he stares straight ahead
Into a scene I cannot imagine

I hear the checkout girl's cheery greeting
His terse "long shift"

As he heads for the door
The downward tilt of his neck

Slumped shoulders
More apparent from behind

I wonder if he will make it to his car
Before opening the bottle

The Edge We Used to Know but Have Forgotten

We had to be with ourselves for awhile
Relearn our heart in the din of stillness
Trail the breath in and out
Unhinge the rusty jawbone

Some days we tried to dance away the lonely
But our feet did not recognize their purpose
Arms swinging like dead logs
Fingers like naughty children refusing to snap

Other days we relished putting our feet up
Savored cookies and wine at odd hours
As if our parents were away
And we the royals we always longed to be

Now something stirs outside our window
That demands attention   That shouts   That flames
Take off the slippers and go to the door
Answer it

PAYING THE RENT

Activism is the rent I pay for living on this planet.
Alice Walker

We swallow the streets;
buildings and lampposts
cannot contain the sea
of signs cresting the crowd.

Arm links arm:
the scars and tattoos, pink hats, dark eyes, mission
mouths, grey hair, broad shoulders, pumped fists,
chanting feet, tie-dye dreamers, middle fingers, moon
dancers, jeweled eyebrows, brother figures, street
hearts, rainbow voices.

We are ironing boards
abandoning closets,
red tulips on the sunny sill,
some mystery novel quickly paced,
a rumpled bed in the afternoon,

and, yes, this rampant force
surging forward,
fear left hollow
in the dust of our footprints.

Planting Beans by the Moon on a Small City Balcony

I'm no Juliet, that's for sure,
though the moon winks like a fat Romeo,

and this twelfth floor stage
offers no earthy base beneath my feet.

Long from the hills I've traveled,
my fingers ache the dark crumble of soil,

that jagged geography of blue jay and hoot owl,
of garden bright and fragrant.

This wide tray gorged with packaged dirt
will have to do for now.

Bean seeds nestle my palm
like warm tiny planets.

I can hear my grandmother:
poke one finger in the soil knuckle deep,

bless the seeds and pat them to bed
like you would tired children,

turn three times against the wind,
then jig as the calling hits you.

Her mountain superstitions ringing
in my ear, I sow my crop,

spin for my waxing Romeo,
hope my neighbors aren't watching

this mad country woman
jigging her love story to the night,

then I wait for the earth to speak:
that voice of green faith rising.

PRAYER FOR THE OLD THINGS

Blessed be my well-thumbed Thesaurus
Its missing Index of x, y, and z
Random pages tea splattered and ink assaulted
What hours spent on the hunt for the perfect word
Like a bloodhound snuffling quarry

Blessed also my metal strainer
Handles dearly departed to some scrap heap
Dented and waffle-faced apparatus
A lifetime of sieving enough spaghetti
To feed all of Italy

Blessings to my alarm clock
Second hand laying dead on the bottom
Like a discarded silver toothpick
Alarm now just a lover's whisper
Nibbling my sleepy ear

And blessed be this spent body
Knees like a rusty gate
Mind a sputtering choke engine
Frayed and graying relic
The ruins of some once-great society

May we find value in what we are
Not in what we lack
May we, like the sun, wake and give light
Flaring our colors wildly
Before we tuck into darkness

Acknowledgments

Special thanks to my family and friends who have always been there when I needed them; all the fantastic folks I've met and worked with through the Carnegie Center for Literacy and Learning; the LexPoMo poets who inspire me year after year after year; my peeps at LPS, PMS+E, book groups, Friday Morning Seniors, and I-Hop for their kind words and encouragement; the decades of people I knew in Metcalfe County; and Larry Moore and everyone at Broadstone Books for making this book possible.

Grateful thanks to the following magazines and journals for printing versions, sometimes with different titles, of my poems:

3 Elements Review — "Eavesdropping on Poets at the Coffee House"
"Fall Carnival"
"How Like a Dumbwaiter is Early Spring"

Agave Magazine — "Zsa Zsa and the Repairman"

Appalachian Heritage (Review) — "And Then There Were Tomatoes"
"Kentucky Crows"
"Patchwork"

Big River Poetry Review — "In the Budding Green"

Black Fox Literary Magazine — "Nothing Was Random"

Bluestone Review — "Sand Hill Cranes"

Crab Fat Literary Magazine — "Window"

Dead Mule School of Southern Literature — "All Day Geese Have Danced"
"Chasing a Little Dog Named Jimmy"

Foliate Oak Literary Magazine — "Zsa Zsa and the Harmony of Puddles"

Elohi Gadugi Journal — "40 Days"

Grasslimb Journal — "40 Days" (Reprint)

Hamilton Stone Review — "Thinking of Aung San Suu Kyi while Smelling the Lilacs"

Heartland Review	"Lullaby Bridge" "What to Love after Daffodils"
Journal of Kentucky Studies	"Flashback Orange" "Inertia, Contemplated" "The Lion and the Lamb" "Stone Ruins, Slater's Field"
Kalliope	"Old Enemies"
Kudzu	"Notes from the Farm" "She Misses"
Lingerpost	"Chiaroscuro"
The Meadow	"Blackberries"
Nuclear Age Peace Foundation website	"To the Boy I Remember, the Man I Grew to Love"
Parnassus Literary Journal	"Deviations"
Perceptions	"Cold Coffee"
Phase and Cycle	"Noisy Birds"
Pikeville Review	"An Old Revolutionary Gets Through Winter" "Circe in October"
Pine Mountain Sand & Gravel	"Deconstructing the Goodbye House"
Poem	"The Dissonance of Mugwort"
The Poetry Box	"Planting Beans by the Moon on a Small City Balcony"
Potato Eyes	"The Sage on This Raw Day Reminds Me of William Faulkner"
Right Hand Pointing	"Petal, Falling"
Scapegoat Review	"Forget Your Sunday Morning Deer"
Silver Threads, Vol. 26	"Crocus in Snow"

Snail Mail Review	"Chicory Blues"
Split Rock Review	"Return To Slater's Pond"
Still: The Journal	"Climb" "Common Wealth" "Huddled Masses" "Light and How It Falls Through Windows" "Nature's Child" "The Room Upstairs"
Third Wednesday	"A Rest of Peaches"
The Tipton Poetry Journal	"A Government of Snow" "The Plumb of Forgetting" "Paying the Rent"
Trickster	"Heat"
Workhorse Publishing Website (Lexington Poetry Month)	"And Then One Day She Lost Poetry" "More like Wolf and Wild Oregano" "On Going Back Again" "Prayer for the Old Things" "Songs in the Key of Darkness" "Telling Myself a Bedtime Story" "The Edge We Used to Know but Have Forgotten" "Wild, Lately"

"The Plumb of Forgetting" was nominated for a Pushcart Prize.

"To the Boy I Remember, the Man I Grew to Love" was a finalist in the Nuclear Age Peace Foundation Competition.

"What to Love after Daffodils" was a finalist in the 2019 *Still: The Journal* Poetry Contest and a finalist in the 2020 *The Heartland Review* Joy Bale Boone Poetry Contest.

About the Author

Allison Thorpe left Wisconsin in the 1970s, traveled around the country, and ended up in Metcalfe County, KY, where she homesteaded for almost four decades. She has published work in a wide variety of journals, received several creative writing grants, and been nominated for two Pushcart Prizes. Her dream is to become an international poker player, smoke signal aficionado, or first-time novelist, whichever comes first. She now lives in Lexington, Kentucky.